Traveling in Company

Poems by
Gene G. Bradbury

BookWilde Children's Books Plus

Traveling in Company
Poems by Gene G. Bradbury
Copyright ©2013 by Gene G. Bradbury

ISBN: 978-0-9897585-0-5

Printed in the United States
by Createspace Independent Publishing Platform

Book design/prepress: Kate Weisel, weiselcreative.com

All inquiries should be addressed to
BookWilde Children's Books Plus
422 Williamson Rd.
Sequim, WA 98382
www.genegbradbury.com

Dedication

This book is dedicated to my wife who has been my traveling companion for over forty years. Without her my life would have been lacking in all that matters most.

Preface

We never begin our journey alone, but are linked by birth to others. They have walked before us and we follow in their footsteps. Those we come to know best on our travels we call family. From them we learn how to live.

Others we meet along the way may lead us to quiet paths of reflection and spiritual practice. We owe them thanks for teaching us how to travel in a beautiful but often complex world. While our journey begins in childhood, it ends after we have gathered memories from our travels. At some point the road narrows for each of us and we come to the place where we must walk alone. The journey ends where it begins. This book of poetry reflects that journey

The eight photographs in this volume are gathered from the 1940s and 1950s. They suggest another time when travel was simpler. In black and white they convey a period of less complexity when there seemed fewer questions and more definite answers. These poems invite us to look back from where we have come in order to better travel the road ahead.

Contents

Other Footprints

Others walk before us.
We follow in their footsteps.

Kansas Henry

He lived in past-tense,
face bleared now by hot steam,
coffee poured into his cup.

Henry pointed his pipe at me,
back-traveled seven decades
to the photo on the glory-wall.

The old soldier stands, steps
like a crooked stovepipe
to his hill of transfiguration.

There in sepia tones, Henry hears
a distant bugle calling formation,
two hundred mounted cavalry.

Sees himself, seated mid-row,
like Teddy Roosevelt on his horse.
"That's me in 1918," he grins.

"Doctors sent me home to die.
Mustard gas coated my lungs.
Outlived them all," he chortles.

Steam disappears in sunlight.
Henry folds himself into a chair.
I lift my cup to Kansas Henry.

Lament

It's gone now, like a quarter
in a magician's handkerchief,
demolished like T.E. Scott's house
by order of the Town Council.

Gone, like lost keys, searched for,
not where they're supposed to be.
Lost like the young boy's body
in the old man's pajamas.

Track of pasture, woodland orchard,
swamp, marked by the Carlisle road,
where Thoreau saw blue laurel buds,
his mind wandering over wild meadows.

Concord, Walden, forever changed,
filled, stuffed, built upon
sold, bought, divided, and taxed
like a convenience store corner.

Thoreau still wanders there,
gazing over Mason's Pasture,
smelling pitch pine,
standing like a memory of then.

Quiet Dust

There drifts a quiet dust
settling softly
over Kansas farms
much as it did one
hundred years ago
when farmers drove
wagons of winter wheat
to granaries in Salina.

Dust from farmer hands
washed away
at the end of day
in the wash room
near the kitchen
where the wheat
has come home
to rest on the table in
sweet smelling bread.

A Small Study

Enter the small study
out of spring rain.
Let quiet visitors,
distant friends,

fall from bookshelves,
to speak of times past,
conversations beneath
fogged window panes.

Henry, from his cabin,
John Muir from the woods,
Charles at Down House,
Nathaniel in the Old Manse,

find their way to this
quiet bookish place,
talk once again beneath
fogged window panes.

Reading William Stafford

It's black out the kitchen window.
I pour the dark night into my coffee cup,
think of William Stafford, waking
at 4:30 every morning to lie on his couch
to dip his bucket into the poet's well.

How daring to be a singular self,
unconcerned with fame or what
starts engines, oils gears, stirs,
frightens, propels us from our beds
to become commuters in life.

I listen to William Stafford's poetry,
butter on toast, hot from the toaster,
content with morning silence,
welcoming words, being there
to write a poem at 4:30 a.m.

Promised Lives

Millions live unsung lives,
hourglass crystals spilled
through time, unlike Jesus
or Buddha, known to all.

Who remembers Soupy Sales,
Renfrew of the Royal Mounties?
Was Michelangelo an angel?
Did Crazy Horse win the Derby?

"You will number the sands,"
Abraham's promise.
Walk barefoot on the beach,
past lives underfoot;

anonymous we return,
grains of ocean sand
washed by waves, unless
a child comes, pail in hand,

to scoop us up, pour the sea water
upon our castle parapets, and
we are remembered yet again
Renfrew, Soupy, Michelangelo,

dry souls on sandy beaches,
risen again in molded form,
to confirm resurrection day,
when grains of sand are child's play.

Traveling With Family

It's the stops along the way we remember:
the births, weddings, celebrations,
and growing old.

Baptism

Remember
    granite rocks
carved from above
shaped by water.

Remember
    wetness spilled
over a child
cleansed by promise,

set free to be the river.

First Love

Don't tell me it wasn't real;
only infatuation, you say.
Love does not come
to one so young.

There is laughter in your voice,
plundering my mind,
a miner, digging deeper,
casting youth aside.

Her name was real, Judy;
I tell you this before you dig.
She was my first love,
my heart cracked open.

I was seven. Don't smile
beneath your miner's hat;
or tell me she was not
a lovely precious stone.

Yes, others followed,
love discovered again,
and again, and again,
through suffering and pain.

One learns how to love
to probe dark recesses
on bended knee, to find
the one last and perfect gem.

Don't tell me this is false,
that it did not begin with her;
love held by the hand, new,
leading at last ...

to you.

Silver Thimble, Golden Thread

A golden needle I will hold
pull it through clouds of gold,
when sun sets I will have
a silver pillow, golden thread.

I'll lift my silver thimble high
sing a song to you and I,
fill it full with wine's red hue
drink a toast from me to you.

All The Little Things

On a thirty-third anniversary

I remember an old farm gate,
white metal, rusted hinges,
placed to keep intruders out.

Your love, like that gate,
holds against unwanted guests:
jealousy, envy, anger.

Little things find a way in,
tenderness, caring, quiet love,
things marriages are made of.

Empathic Listener

Listen to river-rain,
   silent-waiting,
   flowing-pain,
   one who...
stands at the river's edge.

Feel moment's indecision,
   interior spray,
   water's dark passing,
   silent flow, divine prayer,
standing, listening, waiting.

Stay in the moment,
   let shadows pass,
   feel the wet grace
   in silence, hearing,
build a bridge, a place to walk.

The Quiet of Snow
Hannah's birthday, 2010

I am writing poetry today
and you are twenty-six.
I wonder if
the light falling snow
can speak for me, and say. . .

May the lightness of white stars
fall upon your days, and bring
beauty to your life, not
in heavy blizzard or blinding light,
but quiet upon your face.

It will say, stretch out your arms,
open your hands to the sky,
catch each gentle flake
fresh upon your eyes,
and know how precious life is.

Star Weaver

Travels in England

Standing beneath stars,
a timeless weaver's thread
pulled us to Shillingstone,
a place we had not been.

Hands wove us gently
into an English sky
on the walk to Holy Rood,
we strolled there, you and I.

Along the path by starry light,
quilted shadows grew,
gravestones lined the walk,
people we never knew.

We whispered gentle words
beneath celestial sky,
and watched the stars above
light the graves, you and I.

Traveling a Quiet Path

A warm day with a friend.
A garden path. A quiet place.

Early Morning

Before light
hunts the day,
before morning sings,
before a child's fitful cry,
walks a wakeful mother,
to seek a lonely place,
where nothing stirs but she,
and gives herself to quiet
beneath the Linden tree.

Patience

Our toaster
made by turtles,
designed to stall
valuable minutes.

Out the window
snow rests quietly,
on trees limbs,
potting shed roof.

"Breathe, Listen!"
"Smell the toast
cooked by turtles,
slowly...perfectly."

Pearlescence

The prayer class gathered,
circle of uplifted faces,
pearl necklace,
strung by invisible thread.

Each, a speck of
Abraham's promised sand,
birthed from single grains,
Jewels of bright thought.

It snowed in the city,
round crystal flakes,
landing on wet tongues,
lifted to heaven.

Quiet, brilliant, numberless
white stars, floating down
frozen pearls from above,
silent angel messengers.

Indoors we listened,
linked by words, waiting for
prayer to fall quiet as snow,
when the thread broke,

spilled pearls from chairs,
bounced across floor,
out classroom door,
into winter's night.

We looked into a snowy sky
a pearl rosary, mouths open,
received divine grace,
pearlesence, eternal shine.

Still Night

From still night
enter day's
quiet paths,
pointing,
whispering:

Walk in peace.
  Walk in silence.
    Walk in stillness.

From still day
comes night's
quiet paths,
pointing,
whispering:

Sleep in peace
  Sleep in silence
    Sleep in stillness.

Church Bells

Pealing bells,
hollow sounds,
empty pews,
now unpolished,
hallowed halls,
past voices raised
from the loft
hymns of praise.

Night visitors
peer in windows,
empty aisles,
unlit lamps;
seek the living
and forgiving,
carved now
in stony damp.

In the field,
barbed wire fences
guard the graveyard
from the sheep;
they who heard
church bells ringing
now lie down
in sacred sleep.

Tears Like Rain

I will stand in rain
under dark clouds,
gather the tears
of those far away;
feel their wet-weeping
run down my face,
for who can deny
that we, like they,
live under like sky.

When in suffering
my own tears are shed,
I'll look to the clouds
passing high overhead,
let my weeping
be carried aloft, to
drop as rain
on those far off,
who share like pain.

Behold the Stars Beholding You

Where the asphalt ends
grass begins,
winter spruce whispers,
"Look up, see the stars,
beholding you."

When all seems dark
remember, stars are not lost.
Look deeply,
sorrow burns up
in their light.

The distant stars
invite you
to sit at their hearth fire,
be warmed in the night
by their light.

Where the asphalt ends
grass begins,
when all is dark,
behold the stars
beholding you.

Grace of Day

When quiet spoke
the Aspen tree
blown by westerly wind;
I raised my eyes
to falling leaves,
    and then,
    and then,
saw autumn light
through filtered sky
skate shadows
on the ground,
    and then,
    and then,
I showered beneath
drifting wings of
parchment butterfly.

Nature's Way

In the most desolate places
we are never alone.

A Single Moment

In a single moment
early mountain light
crochets doilies
over forest floor.

An old man rocks
on his porch, head bobbing,
a rider on camel-back
weaving over sleeping sands.

A squirrel leaps,
flies through sky,
Garibaldi's high-wire act
without a net.

All in a single moment.

Dungeness

Cumulus clouds sail,
flagships from Spain.
Hulls sweep windy seas,
anchor in Dungeness Bay.
Sound surf's kettle drums
pound breaking waves.

Ancient fleets shimmer
amid suns closing rays.
Dusk filtered sails
fade to bone-yard gray,
casting shadows
over distant quay.

Indian Slough

We pick our way
over graveled paths,
parading along eelgrass
on salt-water marsh.

Step between wet-worlds,
salt water, estuary
surf-soaking mud-flats,
where copepods grow.

Sandpiper clowns point
needle beaks in sand,
pecking their way
over Indian Slough.

Feathered Congregation

In my backyard
a congregation gathers
   raucous crow
   timid quails
   flitting sparrows
   faithful robins
to sing in cacophonous chorus
fowl personalities,
feathered saints.

This Moment's Beauty

The yellowtail butterfly
alights on my window.

A sparrow's song comes
in sips like coffee.

The birding book
opens its wings.

Autumn leaves settle
in thick cups of grass.

Mendelsohn plays,
Songs without Words.

Smoke lifts garden ash
in praise of day.

This moment's beauty.

The Eagle

Two hours he sat,
cocky juvenile,
smug, imperial,
king of snag.

Two hours he sat,
crow-pestered,
blue jay-taunted,
oblivious, Lethe.

Two hours he sat,
sallow eyes, piercing,
unperturbed, undaunted,
throne bird.

A cold-hearted monarch,
a single flutter, no more,
one vociferous objection,
benign ruler.

Cloud Travel

Blow summer breeze
down tracks of sky,
lift me to cloud's
mythical space, where I

ride cumulus white cars,
stowed away, to glide
over ranges of green grass,
skies of silent misty gray.

I'll roll over ancient
grazing shadow shapes,
where once roamed
herds of bison grace.

Thunder

He mumbled moving off
on his way to bed
growing silent in distant light.

His night-shirt swept
the prairie, brushed the sky,
and whispered, good-night.

The Way It Was

Take away
distant tractor,
roofer down hill,
voices on the river,
an old school bell.

Take away
voices, song, breath,
hear the prairie quiet,
finches in trees,
stillness of a heron,
buzz of many bees.

Bird, Seed, Water, Child

Crow drops her acorn,
strikes a muddy bank.

Seed sprouts its ages,
wooden arms to shape.

Water brings the child
to climb its gnarled hips.

Bird, seed, water, child,
cycle is complete.

Traveling with Children

Road trips make childhood memories,
mileposts for later life.

A Safe Place

Her old eyes watched
from nine-paned windows,
as the boy peddled by.
Old dog wagged his tail,
"my boy, my boy."

She sees them halt at
an imaginary stop sign;
observes the dog heel until,
on green, the boy
peddles fast toward

Mr. MacGregor's garden,
Peter Rabbit's nemesis.
The boy draws a
Roy Roger's six-shooter.
Old dog growls.

MacGregor scared inside
the garden shack,
a cap-gun, snarling canine,
and old eyes watching
from nine-paned windows.

Eagle's Eyes

Eagle's eye watched
from atop cedar stem,
child, now five,
hand in father's hand.

Did eagle know
she was a naturalist,
$1.19 binoculars
below cedar stem?

The child watched
eagle preening there.
Her eyes tiptoed to the center,
he ignored her dancing there.

The Moon Prince

When moon's an empty rocking chair,
the Moon Prince comes
to seal childhood dreams,
lest they be left behind.

The Moon Prince flew to me,
robed in moss, lichen hair,
skating forest glade, mallard fair,
leaving wing-prints in the air.

In lake-time, Prince a meal prepared,
of herbs and mushrooms tender care.
He offered me the nectar cup
to drink forever childhood dreams.

My friend would not,
left behind secret places,
let go inner-child to be,
for a bureaucratic plunge.

We meet now on winter's eve.
I bring stories from the wind.
He winds his watch in the night.
I speak of eagles I have seen.

To my earthly child heart unsealed
I pray, when the moon is right
the prince will come, prepare the meal,
give the cup, to seal the heart,
to save the child within.

Meandering

Bent at the hips
   as two-year-olds do,
nose to ground
bloomers in air
   she smells yellow dandelions
     sniffs its yellow eye.

   Wanderers walk crooked,
     curious to see,
roses along fence-lines,
   caterpillar's fur.
     She catches ladybug
landed on her knee.

   Time is a toddler's world,
parents wait, patiently
   her eye pressed to the hole on the bridge
     watching river water
       flow slowly by.

When I Was Nine

When I was nine, Grandpa
winked a devilish wink,
said, "Let's go gallivanting,
you and me. It's a dandy
day for an outing."

"Skeedattle now," said he.
My hand in his,
off to the hush-hush place
to be surprised on this,
a jim-dandy day.

We picked our way through
school auditorium,
balcony's last row seats.
"What will it be, Grandpa?"
I fixed my eyes on the stage.
"Look there," he whispered.
Curtains parted, his hand
slapped his knee, Gene Autry
on Champion rose in the lights,
"a jim-dandy day."

Where Mushrooms Grow

She was seven
and showed us where mushrooms grow,
through woods,
over decaying log,
in shadows by the brook.

"Puffballs," she called them.
Her mushroom book still at home,
she remembered
how they looked
in the wild.

She ran to find us, excited,
led us through wet trees,
over rotting logs,
on until we saw them
growing together as mushrooms do.

In the shadows by the brook,
she captured us,
as mushrooms captured her
to sketch them in her book
like Beatrix Potter.

Traveling Alone

Traveling in company is best, but there
comes a time to travel alone.

Spent Monarch

Seventy years now, king
upon this body's throne;
a Monarch in true flight,
waiting to migrate home.

One morning I'll sweep the air,
let sun glisten off my wings,
tell of miles I have flown,
times and places I have known.

When evening light is right,
in flight spent all my worth,
I'll fold my wings one last time,
falling gently to the earth.

A Golden Light

There is a place,
the end of the road;
leaves are changing,
but not quite all,
giving golden light
to a golden fall.

Near the river,
sits the house where I'll stay
reading and thinking
in halcyon days,
I'll sit in a chair by
a yellow glass lamp,
a golden light
in the autumn damp.

The End of the Journey

Life is part of the adventure,
not the end of the road.

GENE G. BRADBURY writes from his home in the Pacific Northwest where he lives with his wife, Debbie. His writing encompasses poetry, short stories, children's stories and education material for adults. He has self-published three children's books: *The Mouse with Wheels in His Head, The Mouse Who Wanted to Fly,* and *Mischievous Max, A Teddy Bear Story.* His publications may be found in various children's magazines and adult periodicals. Gene teaches adult classes in theology in his area.

Gene has a B.A. in Philosophy, an M.Div. in Theology, and a Master's Degree in Spiritual Direction. Among his many interests he includes books and reading. He and Debbie collect books. A visit to their home is like a visit to a library. Gene is presently working on another children's picture book, a middle-grade chapter book, and a book of short stories. He is involved in numerous writers' workshops and enjoys sharing his stories during school visits.

BookWilde Children's Books

Visit the author's website:

genegbradbury.com

Made in the USA
Charleston, SC
01 February 2014